SPIRITUAL WARFARE DEVOTIONS

Pray, Trust, and Stand Strong

FOR STRENGTH, PROTECTION, AND PEACE

Published by Rosewood Editions

Printed in the United States of America
First Edition: September 2025

CONTENTS

BEFORE YOU BEGIN

*"Put on the full armor of God, so
that you can take your stand..."* —
Ephesians 6:11

Before the ink meets your heart,
before the prayers rise like incense,
pause.

The morning breaks,
but the battle is ancient.
You are not alone in this silence.
He who called you is faithful.

Let the Word be your sword,
let trust be your shield,
let peace be your path.

This is not just a book.
It is a beginning.

THE CALL TO STAND STRONG IN FAITH

In the quiet moments before dawn, when the world still sleeps and darkness gradually yields to light, there exists a sacred space where the soul meets its Creator. It is in these moments, and countless others throughout our days, that we engage in the most profound reality of our existence: the spiritual realm that surrounds our physical world. This devotional book is an invitation to enter that sacred space with intentionality, armed with the power of prayer and the unchanging truth of God's Word.

The apostle Paul, writing to the church in Ephesus, provides us with a sobering yet empowering truth that serves as the foundation for our journey together:

> *"Finally, be strong in the Lord and in his mighty power. Put on the full armor of God, so that you can take your stand against the devil's schemes. For our struggle is not against flesh and blood, but against the rulers, against the authorities, against the powers of this dark world and against the spiritual forces of evil in the heavenly realms." (Ephesians 6:10-12, NIV)*

These words pierce through the veil of our everyday experiences to reveal a truth: we are engaged in a spiritual battle whether we acknowledge it or not. The struggles we face—the anxieties that keep us awake at night, the temptations that pull at our hearts, the discouragements that weigh down our spirits, the conflicts that strain our relationships—these are not merely psychological challenges. They are manifestations of a deeper spiritual reality, a cosmic conflict between the kingdom of light and the forces of darkness.

Yet, this revelation should not lead us to fear but to a place of divine empowerment. For the same God who reveals the reality of spiritual warfare also provides us with everything we need to live in victory. Through prayer, we access the throne room of heaven. Through faith, we activate the power that raised Christ from the dead and now dwells within us.

In our contemporary world, where the pace of life accelerates with each passing year and the noise of countless voices competes for our attention, the need for spiritual grounding has never been more critical. We face challenges our ancestors could never have imagined: the information overload that clouds our discernment, the relativism that questions absolute truth, and the materialism that promises satisfaction but delivers emptiness. These modern manifestations of ancient spiritual battles require us to be more intentional than ever in our spiritual disciplines.

This devotional book is designed to be your companion in this journey of spiritual strengthening. It is not merely a collection of prayers to be recited or passages to be read, but rather a guide to developing a lifestyle of spiritual warfare through prayer, meditation on Scripture, and practical application of God's truth. Each chapter addresses a specific area where believers commonly face spiritual challenges, providing biblical insight, heartfelt prayers, and practical wisdom for standing strong in faith.

The prayers contained within these pages are not rigid scripts that must be followed verbatim. Instead, they are launching points for your own conversations with the Father. As you read and pray through these words, allow the Holy Spirit to personalize them, to expand upon them, and to lead you into deeper communion with the Lord.

As you embark on this devotional journey, approach it with expectancy. God's Word promises that when we draw near to Him, He draws near to us. He is not a distant deity, unconcerned with our daily struggles. He is Emmanuel, God with us, aware of every challenge we face and capable of providing the strength, wisdom, and peace we need. The same Jesus who calmed the storms on the Sea of Galilee stands ready to speak peace into the tempests of our lives. The same Spirit who empowered the early church to transform the world dwells within us today, ready to release that same transformative power in and through our lives.

This book is structured to provide you with a comprehensive toolkit for spiritual warfare. Each chapter begins with a key Scripture passage that serves as the biblical foundation for the theme. The devotional reflections that follow unpack these truths, providing context, application, and encouragement. The prayers offer language and structure for bringing these specific needs before God, while the reflection questions at the end of each chapter invite you to personally engage with the material and apply it to your unique situation.

Use this devotional in whatever way best serves your spiritual growth. Some may choose to read one chapter per day, allowing time for deep meditation and prayer. Others might turn to specific chapters as needs arise, using this book as a reference guide for particular spiritual battles. There is no wrong way to engage with this material, as long as you approach it with an open heart and a sincere desire to grow in your faith.

Remember, spiritual warfare is not about our strength but about God's power working through us. It is not about perfection but about dependence. It is not about never falling but about always getting back up. As you journey through these pages, you will discover that the God who calls us to spiritual battle is the same God who has already secured the victory.

Through Christ's death and resurrection, the ultimate battle has been won. Our daily spiritual warfare is simply the out-working of that victory in our personal lives and spheres of influence.

OPENING PRAYER FOR COURAGE AND SPIRITUAL READINESS

Almighty God, Commander of heaven's armies, I come before You with a heart that longs to know You more deeply. As I begin this journey through Your Word and into deeper realms of prayer, prepare my heart and mind for what You want to reveal.

Lord Jesus, You have conquered sin and death and triumphed over every power of darkness. I acknowledge that apart from You, I can do nothing, but through You, all things are possible. Grant me courage to face spiritual battles not with fear but with confidence in Your victory. Strengthen my faith to stand firm against the enemy's schemes. Give me discernment to recognize truth from deception.

Holy Spirit, be my Guide through every page of this devotional. Open my eyes to see, my ears to hear, and my heart to receive Your truth. Transform these words from text on a page into living truth that changes my life.

Father, I surrender every area of struggle to You. I release my tendency to fight in my own strength and my need to understand everything before I trust. Replace my weakness with Your strength, my fear with Your perfect love. Equip me with Your spiritual armor—truth, righteousness, peace, faith, salvation, and Your Word—that I might stand victorious in battle.

I pray also for every person who will read these pages. Meet them where they are. Speak to their specific battles and struggles. Let this devotional spark spiritual breakthrough and draw us all into deeper intimacy with You.

I declare this to be a season of spiritual victory. No weapon formed against me shall prosper. Greater is He who is in me than he who is in the world.

With expectancy and faith, I begin this journey. In the mighty name of Jesus Christ, my Lord and Savior, Amen.

CHAPTER 1: TRUSTING GOD IN THE MIDST OF UNCERTAINTY

KEY SCRIPTURE

"Trust in the Lord with all your heart and lean not on your own understanding; in all your ways submit to him, and he will make your paths straight." (Proverbs 3:5-6, NIV)

DEVOTIONAL REFLECTION

Life has a way of disrupting our carefully laid plans. Just when we think we have charted our course, unexpected storms arise, familiar landmarks disappear, and we find ourselves navigating through fog so thick we can barely see our next step. In these moments of uncertainty, when the future feels unclear and our human understanding fails us, we face a fundamental choice: will we lean on our limited perspective, or will we trust in the unlimited wisdom of our sovereign God?

The Scripture before us today is perhaps one of the most quoted yet least practiced passages in all of God's Word. Solomon, the wisest man who ever lived, distills divine wisdom into a principle that challenges every fiber of our self-reliant nature. To trust in the Lord with all our heart means to place the full weight of our confidence not in our abilities, resources, or understanding, but in the character and promises of God. It means acknowledging that there is One whose perspective transcends time, whose knowledge encompasses all possibilities, and whose love for us surpasses our deepest comprehension.

Consider for a moment the phrase "lean not on your own understanding." In Hebrew, the word translated as "lean" carries the image of placing one's full body weight upon something, like leaning against a wall for support. How often do we find ourselves leaning heavily on our own ability to figure things out, to predict outcomes, to control variables? We analyze, strategize, and agonize, believing that if we could just think hard enough or plan thoroughly enough, we could eliminate uncertainty from our lives. Yet God invites us into a radically different posture—one of humble dependence upon His infinite wisdom.

Uncertainty is not a sign of God's absence but often an invitation into deeper trust. Throughout Scripture, we see God leading His people through seasons of uncertainty to develop their faith and reveal His faithfulness. Abraham was called to leave everything familiar and journey to an unknown land. Moses stood before the Red Sea with no visible way forward. David spent years in wilderness caves, uncertain when God's promise of kingship would be fulfilled. Mary pondered the angel's announcement, not understanding how God's plan would unfold. In each instance, uncertainty became the canvas upon which God painted His masterpiece of providence.

Uncertainty takes many forms. Perhaps you're facing a career transition, unsure of which direction to take. Maybe you're waiting for medical test results, and the unknown feels unbearable. You might be in a relationship that seems to be at a crossroads, or watching a child make decisions that fill you with concern for their future. Financial pressures might have you wondering how you'll make it through the month, let alone plan for the years ahead. The global landscape shifts rapidly—economic uncertainties, social upheavals, technological disruptions—leaving us feeling unmoored and anxious about what tomorrow might bring.

Yet in the midst of all this uncertainty, God's faithfulness remains unshakeable. He is the same yesterday, today, and forever. The God who guided Israel through the wilderness with a pillar of cloud by day and fire by night still leads His people today. The methods may look different, but His commitment to guide, protect, and provide remains unchanged. When we submit to Him in all our ways—not just in the spiritual compartments of our lives but in every decision, every relationship, every concern—He promises to make our paths straight. This doesn't mean the path will always be easy or that we'll always understand the route, but it means we can trust the One who leads us.

Trusting God in uncertainty requires us to release our death grip on control. It means acknowledging that our perspective is limited to what we can see, while God sees the entire tapestry of history and eternity. We see the tangled threads on the back of the embroidery; He sees the beautiful pattern emerging on the front. We see the individual puzzle pieces scattered and confusing; He sees the completed picture in all its glory. This shift in perspective doesn't come naturally to us. It requires intentional cultivation through prayer, meditation on Scripture, and conscious choices to trust even when we don't understand.

The beautiful promise embedded in this passage is that God will make our paths straight. This doesn't mean our paths will be without obstacles or challenges, but rather that God will guide us through them with purpose and direction. A straight path in biblical terms is not necessarily the shortest or easiest route, but the one that leads us to God's intended destination for our lives. Sometimes God's straight path leads through valleys of shadow, across deserts of testing, or up mountains of difficulty. But each step is purposeful, each turn is intentional, and the destination is always good because our God is good.

Living in trust during uncertainty also means embracing the reality that faith often requires us to take the next step before we can see the whole staircase. God rarely reveals His entire plan at once. Instead, He gives us just enough light for the step we're on, inviting us to trust Him for the next one. This incremental revelation keeps us dependent on Him, maintains our spiritual vitality, and develops the faith muscles we'll need for future challenges. Like manna in the wilderness that couldn't be stored up but had to be gathered daily, God's guidance often comes in daily portions, teaching us to rely on Him moment by moment rather than racing ahead in our own wisdom.

The invitation to trust God in uncertainty is also an invitation to rest. When we truly trust Someone, we can rest even in the midst of storm. A child sleeping peacefully in their parent's arms during a thunderstorm illustrates this principle beautifully. The storm hasn't changed; the child's trust in their parent's protection allows them to rest. Similarly, when we trust our Heavenly Father's sovereign care, we can experience supernatural peace even when circumstances remain uncertain. This rest is not passive resignation but active trust—a conscious choice to place our concerns in God's capable hands and to believe that He is working all things together for our good.

As we navigate seasons of uncertainty, we must also remember that God's timing rarely aligns with our preferences. We live in an instant generation, accustomed to immediate answers and quick resolutions. But God often works on a different timeline, one that prioritizes character development over comfort, spiritual growth over immediate gratification, and eternal purposes over temporary ease. What feels like delay to us might be divine preparation. What seems like a detour might be God's protection from unseen danger. What appears to be a closed door might be God's redirection toward something infinitely better.

PRAYER FOR TRUST IN GOD'S GUIDANCE

Heavenly Father, Sovereign Lord over all creation, I come before You acknowledging my deep need for Your guidance in this season of uncertainty. You know the questions that keep me awake at night, the decisions that weigh heavily on my heart, and the fears that whisper lies about the future. Lord, I confess that I have often tried to navigate life's complexities in my own strength, relying on my limited understanding rather than Your infinite wisdom.

Today, I make a conscious choice to trust You with all my heart. I release my need to have all the answers, to see the complete picture, to control every outcome. Instead, I place my confidence in Your character—Your faithfulness that never fails, Your love that never leaves, Your wisdom that never errs. Guide my steps, Lord, even when I cannot see the path ahead. Give me the courage to follow where You lead, even when the way seems unclear. Help me to remember that You are already present in my tomorrow, preparing the way, working all things together for my good and Your glory.

I submit every area of my life to Your lordship—my relationships, my work, my finances, my health, my dreams, and my fears. Make my paths straight according to Your perfect will. When I'm tempted to lean on my own understanding, remind me of Your faithfulness in the past. When anxiety about the future threatens to overwhelm me, anchor me in the truth of

Your promises. Let my life be a testament to the peace that comes from trusting in You completely. In Jesus' name, Amen.

PRAYER FOR SURRENDERING FEAR OF THE UNKNOWN

Almighty God, my Rock and my Refuge, I bring before You the fears that grip my heart when I face the unknown. You see how uncertainty can paralyze me, how the inability to predict or control the future can fill me with anxiety. Lord, I recognize that these fears stem from forgetting who You are—the Alpha and Omega, the Beginning and the End, the One who holds all things together by the power of Your word.

I surrender to You every fear about tomorrow—fear of failure, fear of loss, fear of pain, fear of disappointment, fear of the unexpected. I choose to believe that You are greater than my fears, that Your perfect love casts out all fear, and that You have not given me a spirit of fear but of power, love, and sound mind. Transform my fear into faith, my anxiety into assurance, my worry into worship.

Help me to remember that the unknown is only unknown to me, not to You. You see the end from the beginning. Nothing catches You by surprise. No circumstance is beyond Your control. As I release my fears into Your capable hands, fill me with Your supernatural peace that surpasses all understanding. Let me rest in the knowledge that the God who clothes the lilies and feeds the birds is intimately concerned with every detail of my life. Give me the grace to embrace uncertainty as an adventure of faith, knowing that You are with me always. Through Christ my Lord, Amen.

REFLECTION QUESTION

Where in your life are you struggling to let go of control and fully trust God's plan? What specific step can you take today to surrender this area to His loving guidance?

CHAPTER 2: PRAYING FOR STRENGTH IN SPIRITUAL BATTLES

KEY SCRIPTURE

"So do not fear, for I am with you; do not be dismayed, for I am your God. I will strengthen you and help you; I will uphold you with my righteous right hand." (Isaiah 41:10, NIV)

DEVOTIONAL REFLECTION

There are moments in our spiritual journey when we feel the weight of the battle pressing down upon us with crushing intensity. Perhaps it's a prolonged season of temptation that seems to assault us at every turn. Maybe it's a spiritual dryness that makes prayer feel like shouting into a void. It could be persecution for our faith, relational conflicts that drain our emotional reserves, or internal struggles with doubt, depression, or despair. In these moments, when our strength fails and our resources are depleted, God speaks through the prophet Isaiah with words that have sustained believers through centuries of spiritual warfare.

The context of this promise is crucial for our understanding. God is speaking to Israel during a time of great upheaval and uncertainty. They faced powerful enemies, overwhelming circumstances, and the temptation to believe that their God had abandoned them. Into this darkness, God declares His presence, His relationship, and His power. He doesn't merely offer sympathy from a distance; He promises His personal involvement in their battles.

Notice the progression of God's promise. First, He addresses our two primary emotional responses to spiritual battles: fear and dismay. Fear paralyzes us, while dismay discourages us. Both are natural human responses to overwhelming spiritual opposition. Yet God's first word is about His presence: "I am with you." Before He promises to change our circumstances, He promises His presence in them. The greatest strength in spiritual battle is not found in our own resources but in the reality that the God of the universe stands with us.

Then God establishes the basis for His help: "I am your God." This is not a generic deity offering abstract assistance. This is personal, relational, covenantal language. The God who created galaxies with a word, who holds atoms together by His power, who orchestrates history according to His purposes—this God claims us as His own. Our spiritual battles are not solo endeavors; they are fought within the context of belonging to the Almighty. When we understand whose we are, we gain perspective on what we face.

The threefold promise that follows is comprehensive in its scope. God promises to strengthen us—infusing His divine power into our human weakness. He promises to help us—coming alongside us as our divine ally and advocate. He promises to uphold us—literally, to grasp us firmly with His righteous right hand, the hand of power and honor in ancient imagery. This is not a tentative touch but a firm grip that will not let us fall.

Spiritual battles often manifest in ways our ancestors couldn't have imagined. The digital age has created new battlegrounds for our faith. We face the constant bombardment of worldviews that oppose biblical truth, delivered through screens that never sleep. Social media can become a minefield of comparison, criticism, and conflict. The pace of modern life can leave us too exhausted for spiritual disciplines, while the abundance of entertainment options can numb us to spiritual realities. We battle against addictions that previous generations never faced, struggle with identity issues amplified by cultural confusion, and fight to maintain biblical convictions in an increasingly hostile society.

Yet the truth remains: God's strength is made perfect in our weakness. The apostle Paul discovered this paradox when he pleaded for God to remove his thorn in the flesh. God's response was not removal but grace: "My grace is sufficient for you, for my power is made perfect in weakness." This divine principle turns our understanding of strength upside down. In the kingdom of God, acknowledging our weakness becomes the pathway to experiencing His strength. Our insufficiency becomes the canvas upon which God displays His all-sufficiency.

Consider how this truth applies to specific spiritual battles you may be facing. If you're battling against a besetting sin that seems to defeat you repeatedly, God's strength is available. Not strength to white-knuckle your way to victory, but divine power that transforms desires and renews minds. If you're struggling with doubt, questioning the very foundations of your faith, God's strength can hold you even when your grip on Him feels weak. If you're facing spiritual opposition in your workplace, family, or community, God's strength can enable you to stand firm with grace and truth.

The promise of God's strength doesn't mean our battles become easy or that we'll never experience defeat in individual skirmishes. Even the apostle Paul spoke of being "hard pressed on every side, but not crushed; perplexed, but not in despair; persecuted, but not abandoned; struck down, but not destroyed." The strength God provides often looks like resilience—the ability to get back up when we've been knocked down, to continue believing when circumstances scream otherwise, to maintain hope when darkness seems overwhelming.

This divine strength also manifests as endurance. The Greek word often translated as "patience" or "endurance" in the New Testament literally means "to remain under"—to stay beneath a heavy load without collapsing. This is not passive resignation but active resistance. It's the strength to keep standing when everything within us wants to quit. It's the power to maintain our spiritual disciplines when they feel dry and unproductive. It's the grace to continue loving difficult people, to keep serving when we're unappreciated, to persist in prayer when heaven seems silent.

Furthermore, God's strength in spiritual battles often comes through His people. We were never meant to fight alone. The body of Christ exists, in part, to provide mutual support in spiritual warfare. When we're too weak to stand, others can hold us up. When we're too discouraged to pray, others can intercede for us. When we've lost perspective, others can remind us of truth. Pride often prevents us from admitting our struggles and seeking help, but God's strength is frequently mediated through the encouragement, accountability, and practical support of fellow believers.

As we seek God's strength for spiritual battles, we must also remember that this strength has a purpose beyond our personal victory. God strengthens us not merely for our own survival but for His glory and the advancement of His kingdom. Our victories become testimonies that encourage others. Our endurance becomes a witness to the reality of God's power. Our transformation becomes evidence of the gospel's truth. When we rely on God's strength rather than our own, He receives the glory, and others are drawn to Him.

PRAYER FOR STRENGTH AND RESILIENCE IN TRIALS

Mighty God, my Strength and my Shield, I come before You acknowledging my desperate need for Your power in the spiritual battles I face. You see the struggles that threaten to overwhelm me, the trials that test my faith, and the weaknesses that the enemy seeks to exploit. Lord, I confess that in my own strength, I am insufficient for these challenges. My human resources are depleted, my emotional reserves are empty, and my spiritual strength feels almost gone.

But I stand on Your promise that You will strengthen and help me, that You will uphold me with Your righteous right hand. Pour into me Your supernatural strength that transcends human ability. When I am weak, be my strength. When I am afraid, be my courage. When I am confused, be my clarity. When I am tempted to give up, be my perseverance. Infuse every fiber of my being with Your divine power that enables me to stand firm against every attack of the enemy.

Lord, I ask for resilience that comes only from You—the ability to bounce back from defeats, to learn from failures without being defined by them, to maintain hope in the midst of hardship. Strengthen my spirit to endure long battles, my mind to resist deception, my heart to remain tender despite wounds, and my will to choose Your ways even when they're difficult. Let my life demonstrate that Your grace is sufficient, that Your power is made perfect in weakness, and that nothing can separate me from Your love. In the mighty name of Jesus, Amen.

PRAYER TO FULLY RELY ON GOD'S POWER

Sovereign Lord, Almighty God, Commander of Heaven's Armies, I confess my tendency to rely on my own strength, wisdom, and resources rather than fully depending on Your unlimited power. Forgive me for the times I've fought spiritual battles in the flesh, attempting to achieve spiritual victory through human effort. I recognize that this self-reliance not only leads to defeat but also robs You of the glory that comes when Your power works through human weakness.

Today, I make a conscious choice to fully rely on Your power rather than my own. I surrender my need to be strong in myself. I release my pride that prevents me from admitting my weakness. I let go of the false security that comes from self-sufficiency. Instead, I embrace the beautiful paradox of Your kingdom—that in my weakness, Your strength is revealed; in my surrender, Your victory is achieved; in my dependence, Your power is displayed.

Teach me what it means to be strong in You and in Your mighty power. Show me how to put on the full armor You provide rather than fashioning my own inadequate protection. Help me to stand firm not through determination alone but through divine enablement. When I face spiritual battles today and in the days ahead, remind me that the battle is Yours, that the power is Yours, and that the victory is already secured through Christ. Let me be a vessel through which Your power flows, accomplishing what human strength never could. Through Jesus Christ, my Victor and Lord, Amen.

REFLECTION QUESTION

In what specific area of your spiritual life are you trying to fight in your own strength rather than relying on God's power? What would it look like to fully surrender this battle to Him?

CHAPTER 3: OVERCOMING FEAR WITH GOD'S PEACE

KEY SCRIPTURE

"For the Spirit God gave us does not make us timid, but gives us power, love and self-discipline." (2 Timothy 1:7, NIV)

DEVOTIONAL REFLECTION

Fear is perhaps one of the enemy's most effective weapons against believers. It whispers lies in the darkness, magnifies problems beyond their actual size, and paralyzes us from stepping into God's purposes for our lives. Fear can take many forms—fear of failure, fear of rejection, fear of the future, fear of loss, fear of death, or even fear of life itself. Yet Paul's words to his spiritual son Timothy pierce through the fog of fear with crystal clarity: the spirit of fear does not originate from God. What God gives is radically different—power, love, and self-discipline, a holy trinity of spiritual resources that overcome fear's paralyzing grip.

Paul writes these words to Timothy at a crucial moment. The young pastor faces overwhelming challenges—internal church conflicts, external persecution, and his own natural timidity. Paul himself writes from prison, facing potential execution. The circumstances could not be more conducive to fear. Yet Paul doesn't offer platitudes or positive thinking. Instead, he points Timothy to a fundamental spiritual reality: the nature of what God has placed within him through the Holy Spirit.

The word translated "timid" or "fear" in this passage refers to cowardice or timidity that shrinks back from duty and calling. It's the kind of fear that makes us retreat when God calls us to advance, remain silent when He calls us to speak, or hide when He calls us to stand. This spirit of timidity is incompatible with the Holy Spirit's nature and work in our lives. God has not given us a spirit that cowers but one that conquers.

Instead, God gives us power—the Greek word "dunamis," from which we get "dynamite." This is not mere human strength but divine enablement, explosive spiritual power that can break through barriers, overcome obstacles, and accomplish the impossible. This power raised Christ from the dead and now resides in every believer. When fear tells us we're not strong enough, God's power declares that He is more than sufficient. When fear insists the giant is too big, God's power reminds us that He has defeated greater enemies. When fear whispers that we'll fail, God's power assures us that His strength is made perfect in our weakness.

God also gives us love—not sentimental affection but "agape," divine love that drives out fear. The apostle John tells us that perfect love casts out fear because fear has to do with punishment. When we're secure in God's love, when we truly grasp that nothing can separate us from it, fear loses its grip. Love motivates us to act despite our fears, to serve others even when it's risky, to obey God even when it's costly. Love transforms our perspective from self-protection to self-sacrifice, from preservation to purpose.

The third gift is self-discipline, sometimes translated as "sound mind" or "self-control." This is the ability to think clearly despite emotional turmoil, to maintain perspective despite overwhelming circumstances, to exercise wisdom despite confusion. Fear thrives on chaotic thinking, catastrophic imaginations, and uncontrolled emotions. But God gives us the ability to take our thoughts captive, to focus on truth rather than speculation, to respond rather than react.

In our current moment, fear seems to be reaching epidemic proportions. We live in an age of anxiety, where fear is not only prevalent but often cultivated. News media profits from fear, social media amplifies it, and political discourse weaponizes it. We face legitimate concerns—global instability, economic uncertainty, health crises, social upheaval, environmental challenges, and technological disruptions that reshape society faster than we can adapt. Added to these collective fears are our personal ones—concerns about our loved ones, our health, our purpose, our future.

Yet into this atmosphere of fear, God's peace speaks a different word. His peace is not the absence of problems but the presence of His Spirit within us. It's not dependent on circumstances but on His character. This peace doesn't make sense to the natural mind—it's a peace that surpasses understanding, a supernatural calm in the midst of natural chaos. It's the peace Jesus displayed sleeping in the boat during the storm, the peace Stephen exhibited while being stoned, the peace Paul and Silas demonstrated singing hymns in prison.

This divine peace is both a gift and a choice. God offers it freely, but we must choose to receive and walk in it. This requires intentional practices that create space for peace to flourish. It means filling our minds with God's Word rather than fear-inducing media. It means bringing our anxieties to God in prayer rather than rehearsing them endlessly in our minds. It means choosing worship over worry, gratitude over grumbling, faith over fear.

The path from fear to peace often requires us to face our fears honestly before God. David models this in the Psalms, where he frequently acknowledges his fears before declaring his trust in God. "When I am afraid, I put my trust in you," he writes. Notice he doesn't deny the fear or pretend it doesn't exist. He acknowledges it but then makes a conscious choice to trust God despite it. This honest acknowledgment allows God's peace to address our real fears rather than our religious facades.

God's peace also comes as we learn to distinguish between legitimate concerns that require action and phantom fears that exist only in our imagination. Much of what we fear never comes to pass. We spend countless hours anxious about scenarios that never materialize, problems that never arise, catastrophes that never occur. Jesus addressed this when He told us not to worry about tomorrow, for tomorrow will worry about itself. Each day has enough trouble of its own. This doesn't mean we shouldn't plan or prepare, but it means we shouldn't allow fear of potential future problems to rob us of present peace.

Furthermore, overcoming fear with God's peace often requires us to take action despite our feelings. Courage is not the absence of fear but action in its presence. God repeatedly commands His people to "fear not" and "be strong and courageous," not because the situations aren't frightening but because He is with us in them. Sometimes the path to peace requires us to do the very thing we fear, trusting God to meet us in our obedience. As we step out in faith, we often discover that the reality is far less terrifying than our imagination suggested.

PRAYER FOR COURAGE
AND BOLDNESS

Almighty God, the One who speaks courage into trembling hearts and boldness into timid spirits, I come before You acknowledging the fears that have held me captive. You know the anxieties that steal my sleep, the worries that cloud my days, and the terrors that paralyze my progress. Lord, I confess that I have often allowed fear to have more influence in my life than faith, that I have listened more to fear's lies than to Your truth.

But today, I claim the promise that You have not given me a spirit of fear but of power, love, and self-discipline. Fill me afresh with Your Holy Spirit, who empowers me to face what I fear, to stand when I want to run, to speak when I want to remain silent. Replace my timidity with holy boldness, my anxiety with divine assurance, my cowardice with Kingdom courage. Help me to remember that the same Spirit who raised Christ from the dead lives in me, and that greater is He who is in me than he who is in the world.

Lord, I ask for courage to step into the calling You've placed on my life, even when it feels overwhelming. Give me boldness to share my faith, even when I fear rejection. Grant me courage to make difficult but necessary changes, to have hard conversations, to stand for truth in a culture that opposes it. Let my life be marked not by the absence of fear but by action in spite of it, demonstrating that Your perfect love casts out all fear. In Jesus' mighty name, Amen.

PRAYER TO REST IN GOD'S PERFECT PEACE

Prince of Peace, my Lord and my God, I come to You weary from the battle against fear and anxiety. My mind has been a battlefield where worries wage war against peace, where "what ifs" multiply faster than I can address them, where fear projects catastrophes that may never occur. I'm exhausted from trying to control what only You can manage, from carrying burdens You never asked me to bear, from fighting battles that belong to You.

Right now, in this moment, I choose to enter Your rest. I lay down my fears at Your feet—every anxiety about the future, every regret about the past, every concern about the present. I choose to believe that You are sovereign over every situation that causes me fear. You are not worried, surprised, or overwhelmed. You have not lost control, run out of options, or been caught off guard. What threatens to undo me is fully under Your authority.

Wash over me with Your supernatural peace that surpasses all understanding. Guard my heart and mind in Christ Jesus. When anxious thoughts assault me, help me to take them captive and make them obedient to Christ. When fear tries to regain ground, remind me of Your faithfulness in the past and Your promises for the future. Teach me to rest in Your perfect peace, not because my circumstances are peaceful but because You are my peace. Let me be still and know that You are God, sovereign over nations, sovereign over nature, and sovereign over every detail of my life. Through Christ, the Prince of Peace, Amen.

REFLECTION QUESTION

What specific fear has been dominating your thoughts and stealing your peace? How can you actively choose to surrender this fear to God and embrace His peace today?

CHAPTER 4: GUARDING YOUR HEART AND MIND WITH GOD'S WORD

KEY SCRIPTURE

"Finally, brothers and sisters, whatever is true, whatever is noble, whatever is right, whatever is pure, whatever is lovely, whatever is admirable—if anything is excellent or praiseworthy—think about such things." (Philippians 4:8, NIV)

DEVOTIONAL REFLECTION

The battlefield of the mind is where many of our spiritual victories are won or lost. Our thoughts shape our emotions, our emotions influence our decisions, and our decisions determine our direction. The enemy understands this principle well, which is why he targets our thought life with such persistence and precision. Like a master strategist, he knows that if he can capture our minds, he can control our lives. Paul's instruction to the Philippians provides us with a divine strategy for mental and spiritual warfare—a filter through which every thought must pass, a standard by which every mental meditation must be measured.

Written from a Roman prison cell, Paul's words carry particular weight. He doesn't write from a place of comfort or ease but from circumstances that could easily justify negative thinking, bitterness, or despair. Yet he demonstrates that our thought life need not be dictated by our circumstances. We have been given the authority and ability to choose what occupies our minds, to curate our thoughts according to divine principles rather than allowing them to run wild according to worldly patterns or emotional impulses.

The list Paul provides is not merely positive thinking or mental self-help. It's a comprehensive framework for biblical meditation that aligns our minds with God's perspective. Each quality he mentions serves as a protective barrier against the toxic thoughts that seek to poison our spiritual well-being. When we fill our minds with what is true, there's no room for the enemy's lies. When we focus on what is noble, we're protected from degrading influences. When we meditate on what is right, pure, lovely, and admirable, we create a mental environment where faith flourishes and fear withers.

Consider the profound implications of focusing on truth in an age of deception. We live in what many call a "post-truth" era, where objective reality is questioned, where "your truth" and "my truth" are considered equally valid regardless of facts, where information and misinformation blend into an indistinguishable mixture. The constant barrage of conflicting messages, conspiracy theories, and manipulated narratives can leave us mentally exhausted and spiritually confused. Yet God's Word stands as unchanging truth, a firm foundation for our thoughts when everything else shifts like sand.

The battle for our minds has intensified in the digital age. Our devices deliver a constant stream of information, much of it designed to trigger emotional responses rather than thoughtful reflection. Social media algorithms feed us content that confirms our biases, creates echo chambers of opinion, and often amplifies the negative over the positive. News outlets compete for attention with increasingly sensational headlines. Entertainment saturates our minds with worldviews and values that subtly—or not so subtly—oppose biblical truth.

Without intentional effort to guard our hearts and minds, we become shaped by forces that oppose God's kingdom.

Scripture serves as both sword and shield in this battle. As a sword, it cuts through deception, divides truth from error, and pierces to the heart of matters. As a shield, it protects our minds from the flaming arrows of doubt, despair, and deception that the enemy launches against us. But Scripture's effectiveness in our lives depends on our engagement with it. A sword left in its sheath and a shield left in the armory provide no protection in battle. We must actively wield God's Word, meditating on it day and night, hiding it in our hearts, and applying it to our thoughts.

The process of renewing our minds according to Scripture is not instantaneous but transformational. Romans 12:2 instructs us, "Do not conform to the pattern of this world, but be transformed by the renewing of your mind." This renewal is ongoing, requiring daily attention and intention. It means consciously choosing to reject thought patterns that contradict God's truth and replacing them with biblical thinking. It means taking every thought captive and making it obedient to Christ, not allowing our minds to wander into territories of fear, lust, bitterness, or despair.

Guarding our hearts and minds also requires us to be selective about what we allow to enter through our eye and ear gates. Jesus said, "The eye is the lamp of the body. If your eyes are healthy, your whole body will be full of light. But if your eyes are unhealthy, your whole body will be full of darkness." What we watch, read, and listen to directly impacts our thought life. This doesn't mean we retreat from the world into religious isolation, but it does mean we exercise wisdom and discernment about our mental diet. Just as we wouldn't intentionally consume physical poison, we shouldn't carelessly consume mental and spiritual toxins.

The practice of biblical meditation differs radically from eastern meditation that seeks to empty the mind. Biblical meditation fills the mind with God's truth, turning it over and over like a precious gem, examining it from every angle, applying it to various situations, and allowing it to sink deep into our consciousness. When we meditate on Scripture, we're not just memorizing words but internalizing truth that shapes our worldview, influences our responses, and fortifies our faith.

Consider how different our mental landscape becomes when we filter our thoughts through Paul's criteria. Instead of dwelling on what's wrong in the world, we look for what's true and right. Rather than feeding on gossip and criticism, we focus on what's pure and admirable. Instead of marinating in negativity and complaint, we seek out what's lovely and praiseworthy. This doesn't mean we ignore problems or pretend everything is perfect. It means we choose to view reality through the lens of faith rather than fear, hope rather than despair, God's sovereignty rather than chaos.

The transformation of our thought life also impacts our emotional well-being. Anxiety often stems from dwelling on worst-case scenarios. Depression can be fueled by rehearsing negative thoughts. Anger grows when we meditate on offenses. But when we fill our minds with God's truth, promises, and perspective, our emotions begin to align with His peace. We experience the reality of Isaiah 26:3: "You will keep in perfect peace those whose minds are steadfast, because they trust in you."

Furthermore, guarding our hearts and minds with God's Word equips us to help others in their mental and spiritual battles. When we've learned to combat lies with truth, to replace fear with faith, to overcome negative thinking with biblical meditation, we become equipped to minister to others struggling with similar battles. Our testimonies of mental and spiritual victory become weapons in the hands of fellow believers fighting their own battles.

PRAYER FOR WISDOM
AND DISCERNMENT

All-Knowing God, Source of all wisdom and truth, I come before You acknowledging my need for divine discernment in a world full of deception. You see how the enemy seeks to infiltrate my mind with lies disguised as truth, with fear masquerading as wisdom, with worldly thinking presented as enlightenment. Lord, I confess that I have not always guarded my heart and mind as diligently as I should. I have allowed toxic thoughts to take root, entertained ideas that oppose Your truth, and meditated on things that steal my peace and corrupt my faith.

Grant me, Lord, the wisdom that comes from above—wisdom that is pure, peace-loving, considerate, submissive, full of mercy and good fruit, impartial and sincere. Sharpen my spiritual discernment to recognize the enemy's deceptions no matter how cleverly disguised. Help me to test every thought, every idea, every philosophy against the unchanging standard of Your Word. Give me the courage to reject what is false, even when it's popular, and to embrace what is true, even when it's costly.

Teach me to be a vigilant guardian of my mind, carefully screening what I allow to enter through my eyes and ears. Help me to choose wisely what I read, watch, and listen to, recognizing that these choices shape my thoughts and ultimately my life. When false messages attempt to take root in my mind, let Your Word rise up within me to counter them. When doubt whispers its questions, let Your truth shout its answers. Fill my mind so completely with Your Word that there's no room for the enemy's lies. In Jesus' name, Amen.

PRAYER TO FOCUS ON GOD'S TRUTH AND REJECT LIES

God of all truth, Light of the world, Revealer of hidden things, I bring before You a mind that has too often been influenced by the father of lies. You know the false beliefs I've accepted, the deceptions I've embraced, and the lies I've allowed to shape my identity and decisions. Today, I choose to reject every lie the enemy has planted in my mind—lies about who You are, who I am, and what my future holds.

I specifically reject the lie that I am not enough, replacing it with the truth that I am fearfully and wonderfully made. I reject the lie that my past defines me, embracing the truth that I am a new creation in Christ. I reject the lie that I am alone, standing on the truth that You will never leave nor forsake me. I reject the lie that my situation is hopeless, claiming the truth that with You all things are possible. I reject the lie that I need to earn Your love, celebrating the truth that Your love is unconditional and everlasting.

Fill my mind, Lord, with whatever is true, noble, right, pure, lovely, admirable, excellent, and praiseworthy. Help me to meditate on Your Word day and night, to hide it in my heart that I might not sin against You. Transform my thinking patterns to align with Your thoughts. When lies attempt to resurface, remind me of Your truth. When deception seems convincing, anchor me in Your Word. Let my mind be so saturated with Scripture that Your truth becomes my first thought in every situation. Through Christ, who is the Way, the Truth, and the Life, Amen.

REFLECTION QUESTION

What specific lies or negative thought patterns have you been entertaining that need to be replaced with God's truth? Which Scripture can you memorize and meditate on this week to combat these destructive thoughts?

CHAPTER 5: PRAYING FOR PROTECTION IN TIMES OF DANGER

KEY SCRIPTURE

"Whoever dwells in the shelter of the Most High will rest in the shadow of the Almighty. I will say of the Lord, 'He is my refuge and my fortress, my God, in whom I trust.'" (Psalm 91:1-2, NIV)

DEVOTIONAL REFLECTION

In a world where danger can emerge from countless sources—physical threats, spiritual attacks, emotional assaults, relational betrayals, financial disasters, health crises—the promise of divine protection speaks profound comfort to anxious hearts. Psalm 91 has been the anchor for countless believers facing peril throughout history. Warriors have carried it into battle, parents have prayed it over children, missionaries have claimed it in hostile territories, and ordinary believers have clung to it in extraordinary circumstances. Yet this psalm offers more than just protection; it reveals the intimate relationship between the protected and the Protector.

The opening verse establishes a critical condition: "Whoever dwells in the shelter of the Most High." This dwelling is not a casual visit or emergency retreat but a permanent residence, an abiding presence, a continuous remaining. The Hebrew word implies settling down, making one's home, establishing permanent residence. Protection is not found in occasionally running to God when danger threatens but in maintaining an ongoing, intimate relationship with Him. Those who dwell in His shelter have made the conscious choice to live under His lordship, within His will, and inside the boundaries of His kingdom.

The imagery of shelter and shadow speaks to different aspects of God's protection. A shelter provides structural protection from storms and enemies—it's defensive and strong. A shadow provides relief from scorching heat—it's comforting and refreshing. The Most High God, El Elyon, the One who is sovereign over all, provides both fortress-like protection from external threats and cooling shade from life's exhausting pressures. This is comprehensive coverage for every type of danger we might face.

The personal declaration in verse two transforms theological truth into personal testimony: "I will say of the Lord, 'He is my refuge and my fortress, my God, in whom I trust.'" This is not merely intellectual acknowledgment but vocal declaration. There's power in speaking our trust aloud, in declaring God's protection over our lives, in verbally affirming our confidence in His care. This declaration is both an act of faith and a weapon of warfare, pushing back fear with proclaimed trust.

In our contemporary world, dangers have multiplied and morphed into forms previous generations couldn't have imagined. We face cyber threats that can destroy reputations and steal identities. We encounter social media attacks that assault our emotional well-being. We navigate health threats that emerge and spread globally with unprecedented speed. We deal with economic uncertainties that can evaporate life savings overnight. We confront violence that can erupt anywhere— schools, churches, marketplaces, homes. The evening news catalogs an endless litany of dangers, each story amplifying our sense of vulnerability.

Yet God's protection remains relevant and reliable for modern dangers just as it was for ancient ones. The God who protected Daniel in the lion's den can protect us in corporate board rooms where our faith is challenged. The God who preserved the three Hebrew young men in the fiery furnace can preserve us in the heat of cultural opposition. The God who shielded David from Saul's spear can shield us from attacks both physical and digital. His methods may vary, but His commitment to protect His children remains constant.

It's crucial to understand that God's protection doesn't mean we'll never face danger or difficulty. Scripture is filled with examples of godly people who experienced persecution, suffering, and even martyrdom. God's protection sometimes means preservation from danger, but other times it means preservation through danger. Sometimes He calms the storm; other times He calms His child in the storm. Sometimes He removes the threat; other times He removes our fear of the threat. His protection is always perfect, even when it doesn't match our preferences.

The promise of protection is also not a license for presumption or foolishness. Jesus, when tempted by Satan to throw Himself from the temple pinnacle while quoting Psalm 91, responded that we must not put the Lord our God to the test. Divine protection doesn't mean we can be reckless with our safety, ignore wisdom, or presume upon God's grace. We lock our doors, wear seatbelts, and take reasonable precautions while trusting God for protection beyond our human efforts.

God's protection often extends beyond our individual lives to encompass those we love. Parents pray protection over children, spouses over each other, pastors over congregations, friends over friends. This intercessory dimension of protective prayer reflects God's heart for community and His design for us to bear one another's burdens. When we pray protection over others, we participate in God's protective purposes, becoming instruments of His sheltering care.

The spiritual dimension of protection is perhaps the most crucial yet often most overlooked. Our ultimate dangers are not physical but spiritual. A damaged body is temporary; a damaged soul is eternal. God's protection extends to our spiritual lives, guarding us from deception, preserving us from apostasy, protecting us from the schemes of the devil. He shields our faith when doubts assault, protects our hope when circumstances discourage, and guards our love when offenses multiply.

The invitation to dwell in God's shelter is extended to all, but not all accept it. Some prefer to rely on their own resources, trusting in wealth, weapons, or wisdom for protection. Others acknowledge their need for divine protection but only seek it sporadically, in moments of crisis. But those who have learned to dwell in the shelter of the Most High have discovered a peace that transcends circumstances, a security that surpasses understanding, and a protection that encompasses every aspect of life.

PRAYER FOR GOD'S PROTECTION OVER YOU AND YOUR LOVED ONES

Almighty God, my Shield and Defender, I come under the shelter of Your wings seeking Your divine protection over my life and the lives of those I love. You are sovereign over every force that would threaten our safety. I declare that You are our refuge and fortress.

Lord, I ask for Your protective covering over every area of our lives. Guard our bodies from harm, our minds from deception, our emotions from trauma, and our spirits from the enemy's schemes. Surround our homes with Your angels, our travels with Your safety, our workplaces with Your presence.

I lift up each person in my circle of care—family, friends, neighbors, colleagues. Cover them with Your protective love. Go before them to prepare their way, stand beside them in trials, and guard them from enemy attacks. Where danger threatens, provide escape. Where fear dominates, release Your peace. Let no weapon formed against us prosper.

I trust not in our own ability to protect ourselves but in Your unlimited power and unfailing love. You neither slumber nor sleep, and Your watchful eye is always upon us. Thank You for being our ever-present help in trouble. In the mighty name of Jesus, our Protector, Amen.

PRAYER TO TRUST IN GOD'S SAFETY AND CARE

Faithful Father, Keeper of my soul, I confess that fear often speaks louder than faith in my heart. When I see dangers multiplying, hear of tragedies, or imagine what could go wrong, anxiety threatens to overwhelm my trust in Your care. Forgive me for doubting Your protection and for trying to control what only You can manage.

Today, I choose to trust in Your safety and care, not because danger doesn't exist, but because You are greater than any danger. I believe You are working all things for my good and that nothing touches my life without Your permission. You will either shield me from trouble or strengthen me through it.

Help me rest in Your care like a child sleeps peacefully in their parent's arms. When threats arise, remind me that You are my hiding place. When dangers approach, You are my strong tower. Teach me to dwell in Your protective presence. Let my life testify that You are a faithful Protector who never fails those who trust in You. Through Christ my Lord, Amen.

REFLECTION QUESTION

What specific dangers or threats are causing you the most anxiety right now? How can you practically "dwell in the shelter of the Most High" and trust His protection in these areas?

CHAPTER 6: RELEASING BURDENS THROUGH PRAYER

KEY SCRIPTURE

"Come to me, all you who are weary and burdened, and I will give you rest. Take my yoke upon you and learn from me, for I am gentle and humble in heart, and you will find rest for your souls. For my yoke is easy and my burden is light."
(Matthew 11:28-30, NIV)

DEVOTIONAL REFLECTION

These words of Jesus have echoed through centuries as one of the most tender and compelling invitations ever extended to humanity. Spoken to people crushed under the weight of religious legalism, societal oppression, and personal struggles, Christ's invitation transcends time and culture to reach us in our modern weariness. In a world that constantly demands more—more productivity, more achievement, more perfection—Jesus offers something radically different: rest. Not just physical rest, though that's included, but soul-deep rest that touches the very core of our being.

The invitation begins with a simple yet profound command: "Come." Not "achieve," "accomplish," "improve yourself," or "get your act together first." Simply come. Come as you are, with all your weariness, all your burdens, all your failures and fears. This accessibility of Christ stands in stark contrast to religious systems that demand we climb our way to God through our own efforts. Jesus descends to where we are and invites us to bring our burdens to Him.

The audience for this invitation is specific: "all you who are weary and burdened." The Greek word for weary implies exhaustion from labor, being spent from toiling. The word for burdened suggests being loaded down like a pack animal carrying more than it can bear. Jesus sees us staggering under loads we were never meant to carry—the weight of trying to earn salvation, the burden of others' expectations, the load of past regrets, the heaviness of future anxieties, the crushing weight of unforgiveness, the exhausting burden of maintaining facades.

In our contemporary context, the sources of our weariness have multiplied exponentially. We carry the burden of information overload, knowing too much about too many problems we cannot solve. We bear the weight of constant connectivity, never truly able to rest from the demands of work and relationships. We struggle under financial pressures that previous generations couldn't imagine—student loans, medical debts, housing costs that outpace income growth. We're exhausted from the pace of change, the pressure to keep up, the fear of being left behind.

We also carry relational burdens that wear us down—broken marriages, prodigal children, aging parents, difficult friendships, workplace conflicts. We bear emotional burdens of grief that won't heal, depression that won't lift, anxiety that won't quiet. We struggle with spiritual burdens of doubt, disappointment with God, disillusionment with church, questions that seem to have no answers. Layer upon layer, these burdens accumulate until we can barely function, much less flourish.

Yet Jesus doesn't merely offer sympathy for our condition; He offers transformation of it. "I will give you rest," He promises. This is not rest we must earn or achieve but rest He gives as a gift. It's the rest of cessation from striving, of release from the exhausting effort of self-salvation. It's the rest of reconciliation with God, of peace that comes from knowing we're accepted, forgiven, and loved. It's the rest of surrender, of finally admitting we cannot carry these loads and transferring them to shoulders broad enough to bear them.

But then Jesus presents what seems like a paradox: "Take my yoke upon you." He promises rest but offers a yoke. A yoke is a burden-bearing instrument, yet Jesus calls His yoke easy and His burden light. The mystery resolves when we understand that Jesus isn't calling us to a burden-free life but to an exchange of burdens. We give Him our crushing loads and take on His purposeful yoke. We trade our heavy burden of self-effort for His light burden of grace-empowered obedience. We exchange our exhausting striving for His restful abiding.

The yoke imagery would have been immediately understood by His original audience. A yoke joins two animals together for shared labor. When we take Christ's yoke, we're joined with Him in the work. He bears the weight; we simply walk alongside Him. The experienced, stronger animal bears the majority of the load while training the younger, weaker one. So Christ bears the true weight while we learn from Him, drawing on His strength rather than depleting our own.

"Learn from me," Jesus says, "for I am gentle and humble in heart." This learning is not primarily intellectual but relational and practical. We learn His ways of responding to life's pressures. We learn His rhythm of work and rest. We learn His perspective on what truly matters. We learn His dependence on the Father. We learn that strength can coexist with gentleness, that authority can coincide with humility. In this learning, this discipleship, we find rest for our souls.

The rest Jesus offers is not inactivity but peace in activity. It's not the absence of responsibility but the presence of divine enablement. It's not escape from life's demands but equipment for meeting them. When we're yoked with Christ, we still work, serve, and carry responsibilities, but we do so drawing on His infinite resources rather than our limited reserves. We work from rest rather than for rest. We serve from acceptance rather than for acceptance. We live from love rather than for love.

Prayer becomes the primary means by which we release our burdens to Christ. In prayer, we consciously transfer the weight from our shoulders to His. We verbalize our weariness, acknowledging our inability to carry these loads. We itemize our burdens, specifically handing each one to Him. We confess our tendency to take them back, asking for grace to leave them in His capable hands. Through prayer, the divine exchange takes place—our heaviness for His lightness, our exhaustion for His energy, our anxiety for His peace.

Yet releasing burdens through prayer is often a process rather than a one-time event. Some burdens we've carried so long they feel like part of us. We've grown so accustomed to their weight that we feel naked without them. Some burdens we secretly believe we deserve to carry as punishment for past sins. Others we're afraid to release because they've become our identity—we don't know who we'd be without our struggles. Still others we take back repeatedly, trusting ourselves more than we trust God to handle them properly.

The practice of casting our burdens on the Lord requires both faith and discipline. Faith to believe He cares enough to take them and is capable of handling them. Discipline to resist the temptation to take them back. It requires us to develop new habits of thought and response. When worry arises, we immediately turn it into prayer. When burdens feel heavy, we consciously transfer them to Christ. When weariness overwhelms, we retreat to His presence for renewal.

PRAYER FOR LETTING GO OF WORRY

Loving Father, Prince of Peace, Bearer of my burdens, I come to You weary from carrying loads You never asked me to bear. My shoulders ache from the weight of worries I've accumulated—concerns about tomorrow that rob today of its joy, anxieties about situations beyond my control, fears about outcomes I cannot predict. Lord, I confess that I have often trusted my own ability to worry more than Your ability to work. I have believed the lie that if I worry enough, I can somehow change things, protect myself, or prepare for every possibility.

Today, I accept Your invitation to come and find rest. I choose to release every worry into Your capable hands. I give You my financial concerns, trusting You to provide as You've promised. I release my health anxieties, believing You are the Great Physician who numbers my days. I hand over my relationship worries, knowing You work in hearts in ways I cannot. I surrender my fears about the future, acknowledging that You're already there preparing the way. I let go of my need to control outcomes, recognizing that Your plans are higher and better than mine.

Help me, Lord, to truly let go, not just temporarily set aside these worries only to pick them up again. When I'm tempted to take them back, remind me of Your faithfulness. When new worries arise, help me to immediately turn them into prayers. Teach me to cast all my anxiety on You because You care for me. Replace my worry with worship, my anxiety with adoration, my fear with faith. Let me experience the peace that surpasses understanding as I learn to trust You with everything that concerns me. In Jesus' name, Amen.

PRAYER FOR PEACE AND REST IN GOD'S CARE

Gentle Savior, Giver of rest, Keeper of my soul, I accept Your invitation to exchange my heavy burdens for Your easy yoke. I'm exhausted from trying to be strong enough, good enough, wise enough in my own strength. I'm weary from wearing masks, maintaining appearances, meeting everyone's expectations. I'm tired of striving, achieving, and proving my worth. Today, I lay down these exhausting efforts at Your feet.

I take up Your yoke instead, yoking myself to You in intimate partnership. Teach me Your rhythm of grace, Your pace of peace, Your way of restful productivity. Show me how to work from rest rather than for rest, to serve from love rather than for love, to live from acceptance rather than for acceptance. Help me to learn from You—Your gentleness in dealing with weakness, Your humility in wielding power, Your peace in facing opposition.

Grant me the rest You promise—rest for my body from exhausting striving, rest for my mind from anxious thoughts, rest for my emotions from constant upheaval, rest for my soul from the burden of self-salvation. Let me experience the lightness that comes from walking with You, the ease that flows from depending on Your strength, the peace that results from trusting Your heart. When I'm tempted to pick up my old burdens, remind me of the rest available in You. Let my life demonstrate to others that Your yoke is indeed easy and Your burden truly light. Through Christ my Lord, Amen.

REFLECTION QUESTION

What specific burdens have you been carrying that you need to release to God today? What makes it difficult for you to let go of these burdens, and how can you practice leaving them in His hands?

CHAPTER 7: STANDING FIRM AGAINST TEMPTATION

KEY SCRIPTURE

"No temptation has overtaken you except what is common to mankind. And God is faithful; he will not let you be tempted beyond what you can bear. But when you are tempted, he will also provide a way out so that you can endure it." (1 Corinthians 10:13, NIV)

DEVOTIONAL REFLECTION

In the moment of temptation, when desire pulls with magnetic force and rationalization whispers its convincing lies, we often feel utterly alone and uniquely weak. The enemy wants us to believe that our struggle is exceptional, that others don't face what we face, that our temptation is either too powerful to resist or too shameful to confess. Yet Paul's words to the Corinthians shatter these isolating deceptions with liberating truth: you are not alone in your struggle, you are not without divine help, and you are not destined to defeat.

The first comfort Paul offers is the universality of temptation: "No temptation has overtaken you except what is common to mankind." The struggles that feel so personal, so unique to your situation, are actually part of the common human experience. The businessman tempted to compromise integrity for profit faces the same basic temptation as the student tempted to cheat on an exam—the lure of taking shortcuts to success. The person battling lustful thoughts shares the same fundamental struggle as someone fighting gluttony or greed—the challenge of controlling physical appetites. This commonality doesn't minimize our personal responsibility, but it does remove the enemy's weapon of isolation and shame.

Understanding that our temptations are common to humanity helps us in several ways. First, it means others have faced what we face and have found victory—we're not pioneers in an unexplored wilderness but followers on a well-worn path where others have successfully navigated. Second, it means we can find understanding and support from fellow believers who know our struggle personally. Third, it reminds us that Christ Himself was tempted in every way we are, yet without sin, making Him a compassionate and understanding High Priest who can sympathize with our weaknesses.

The promise that follows is even more powerful: "God is faithful; he will not let you be tempted beyond what you can bear." This divine faithfulness stands as an immovable rock in the shifting sands of temptation. God knows our frame, remembers that we are dust, and measures out exactly what we can handle with His help. This doesn't mean temptation will be easy to resist, but it does mean it's never impossible to resist. Every temptation we face has been filtered through God's protective sovereignty. He has already determined that with His grace, we can overcome it.

Temptations have taken on new forms while retaining ancient roots. Technology has brought temptation into our pockets through smartphones that provide instant access to pornography, gambling, shopping, and countless other potential snares. Social media creates new temptations for comparison, vanity, gossip, and wrath. The pace of modern life tempts us to neglect spiritual disciplines, family relationships, and physical health in pursuit of success. The abundance of options in everything from entertainment to relationships creates temptations previous generations never imagined.

Yet the promise remains: God will provide a way out. This escape route is not always what we expect or prefer. Sometimes it's as simple as physically removing ourselves from a tempting situation. Sometimes it's as difficult as confessing our struggle to another person and asking for accountability. Sometimes it's as practical as installing internet filters or as spiritual as intensive prayer and fasting. The way out might be a Scripture that comes to mind at the crucial moment, a phone call from a friend just when we're about to fall, or a sudden change in circumstances that removes the temptation.

The key phrase is "so that you can endure it." God's provision doesn't always mean the immediate removal of temptation but often the strength to endure it without sinning. Joseph didn't stop being tempted by Potiphar's wife in a single day—he had to endure ongoing temptation, day after day, choosing righteousness each time. Jesus endured forty days of fasting and temptation in the wilderness. The ability to endure temptation without yielding is itself a form of spiritual victory that develops character, strengthens faith, and prepares us for greater challenges ahead.

Standing firm against temptation requires understanding its progressive nature. James tells us that temptation follows a predictable pattern: desire conceives and gives birth to sin, and sin when full-grown gives birth to death. Recognizing this progression helps us identify danger points early. The battle is most easily won at the level of thought, before desire takes root. Once desire is entertained and nurtured, resistance becomes exponentially more difficult. This is why Jesus taught such radical measures—if your eye causes you to sin, pluck it out. Better to deal decisively with temptation at its inception than to fight a losing battle against fully developed sin.

We must also recognize that different seasons of life bring different temptations. The young face temptations related to identity, sexuality, and life direction. Middle age brings temptations of compromise, comfort, and covetousness. Later years can bring temptations of bitterness, regret, and spiritual complacency. Our vulnerabilities shift with our circumstances—success might bring pride, failure might bring despair, isolation might bring destructive habits, relationships might bring unhealthy dependencies. Awareness of our current vulnerabilities helps us guard against specific threats.

It's also vital to understand that victory over temptation is not achieved through willpower alone but through the power of the Holy Spirit. The same Spirit that raised Christ from the dead lives in us, providing supernatural strength to resist temptation. When we walk in the Spirit, we do not gratify the desires of the flesh. This walking involves moment-by-moment dependence on God's grace, conscious yielding to the Spirit's control, and immediate obedience to His promptings. The Spirit provides not just strength to resist but transformation of desires, gradually conforming us to Christ's image so that what once tempted us loses its appeal.

Furthermore, we must prepare for temptation before it arrives. A soldier doesn't wait until battle to prepare weapons and strategy. Similarly, we must prepare for temptation through regular spiritual disciplines. Memorizing Scripture provides weapons for the moment of battle. Regular prayer maintains our connection to the source of strength. Worship reorients our desires toward God. Fellowship provides accountability and encouragement. These practices don't guarantee we'll never be tempted, but they position us for victory when temptation comes.

PRAYER FOR PURITY
AND HOLINESS

Holy God, Righteous Father, Purifier of hearts, I come before You acknowledging the battle for purity that rages within me. You know every temptation I face, every weakness in my armor, every area where the enemy has gained ground in the past. Lord, I confess that I have not always valued holiness as You do, that I have sometimes entertained impurity rather than fleeing from it, that I have relied on my own strength rather than Your power to resist.

Today, I ask for a fresh impartation of Your holiness in my life. Create in me a clean heart, O God, and renew a right spirit within me. Give me eyes that see the true nature of sin—its destructiveness, its deceptiveness, its ultimate emptiness. Help me to hate what You hate and love what You love. Transform my desires so that they align with Your will. Where impure thoughts have taken root, uproot them by Your power. Where unholy habits have formed, break them by Your grace. Where sinful patterns have developed, transform them by Your Spirit.

I ask for practical wisdom in pursuing purity. Show me what situations to avoid, what relationships to reconsider, what habits to change. Give me the courage to take radical steps if necessary—to cut off sources of temptation, to seek accountability, to confess hidden struggles. Help me to remember that the temporary pleasure of sin is never worth the lasting consequences. Fill me with such satisfaction in You that the allure of sin loses its power. Let my life be marked by holiness that draws others to You. In the name of Jesus, who was tempted yet without sin, Amen.

PRAYER FOR DELIVERANCE FROM TEMPTATION

Mighty Deliverer, Strong Tower, Ever-present Help in trouble, I cry out to You from the midst of temptation that threatens to overwhelm me. You see the battle I'm fighting, the pull I'm feeling, the weakness I'm experiencing. Lord, I claim Your promise that You will not allow me to be tempted beyond what I can bear and that You will provide a way out so that I can endure it.

Show me the way of escape You've provided. If it's a door to walk through, give me courage to walk. If it's a conversation to have, give me words to speak. If it's a relationship to end, give me strength to let go. If it's a habit to break, give me power to change. If it's help to seek, give me humility to ask. Open my eyes to see the exit You've prepared, and give me the will to take it even when everything within me wants to stay.

Deliver me not only from this present temptation but from the patterns that lead me into temptation. Show me the triggers that make me vulnerable, the situations that weaken my resolve, the thoughts that begin the downward spiral. Help me to be proactive in avoiding temptation rather than reactive in resisting it. Teach me to pray daily, "Lead us not into temptation, but deliver us from evil," and to live in a way that cooperates with that prayer. Surround me with Your protection, fill me with Your Spirit, and keep me in the center of Your will where temptation loses its power. Through Christ my Lord, who overcame every temptation, Amen.

REFLECTION QUESTION

What recurring temptation are you facing that seems too strong to overcome? How can you actively seek and utilize God's "way out" in this specific area of struggle?

CHAPTER 8: FINDING HOPE IN TIMES OF WAITING

KEY SCRIPTURE

"But those who hope in the Lord will renew their strength. They will soar on wings like eagles; they will run and not grow weary, they will walk and not be faint." (Isaiah 40:31, NIV)

DEVOTIONAL REFLECTION

Waiting is perhaps one of the most difficult disciplines in the spiritual life. We live in an age of instant everything—instant communication, instant information, instant gratification. Yet God often calls us into seasons of waiting that stretch our faith to its limits and reveal the true condition of our hearts. The promise Isaiah delivers to God's weary people speaks directly to those in the waiting room of life, offering not just endurance but transformation, not just survival but supernatural strength.

The context of this promise is crucial. Isaiah speaks to a people in exile, waiting for deliverance that seems impossibly delayed. They're not waiting for luxuries but for liberation, not for preferences but for promises to be fulfilled. Their waiting is tinged with doubt—has God forgotten? Has He changed His mind? Is He unable to deliver? Into this darkness of delay, God speaks through His prophet, reminding them that His timing is perfect, His power is unlimited, and His purposes will prevail.

The Hebrew word translated as "hope" or "wait" carries the sense of stretched expectation, like a rope pulled taut. It's active waiting, not passive resignation. It's expectation stretched over time, maintaining tension without breaking. This kind of hoping/waiting requires spiritual muscle, developing strength we didn't know we needed. It's in the waiting that our faith moves from theory to practice, from confession to conviction, from knowledge about God to experience with God.

Consider the promises attached to this waiting: renewed strength, soaring like eagles, running without weariness, walking without fainting. Notice the progression—from soaring to running to walking. Sometimes in our waiting, God grants moments of soaring, supernatural experiences where we rise above our circumstances on wings of faith. Other times, we're running, making progress, seeing movement, feeling momentum. But often, waiting involves simply walking, putting one foot in front of the other, continuing forward when everything within us wants to quit.

In our experience, waiting takes many forms. Singles wait for life partners, wondering if God has forgotten their desire for companionship. Couples wait for children, each month bringing fresh disappointment. The unemployed wait for job opportunities, watching savings dwindle and anxiety rise. The sick wait for healing, enduring treatments and praying for miracles. Parents wait for prodigal children to return, scanning the horizon daily for signs of homecoming. Dreamers wait for doors to open, watching others seemingly advance while they remain stuck.

The waiting can be excruciating. It can feel like divine silence, cosmic indifference, or spiritual punishment. We watch others receive what we're waiting for and wonder why we're passed over. We see the wicked prosper while we suffer, and questions multiply in our hearts. We pray, fast, believe, and claim promises, yet the waiting continues. It's in these stretched seasons that we discover whether our faith is in God Himself or merely in what we hope He'll do for us.

Yet Scripture is filled with testimonies of those who waited and were not disappointed. Abraham waited twenty-five years for the promised son. Joseph waited thirteen years from pit to palace. Moses waited forty years in the wilderness before his calling was activated. David waited years between his anointing and his throne. The disciples waited in Jerusalem for the promised Holy Spirit. Each waiting season was preparation for greater purpose, though it rarely felt that way in the moment.

God's activity during our waiting is often hidden but always purposeful. He's working in us, developing character that couldn't be forged any other way. Patience, perseverance, humility, dependence—these fruits grow best in the soil of waiting. He's working through us, using our waiting to impact others who are watching. Our response to delay can be a powerful testimony to God's worthiness regardless of circumstances. He's working for us, orchestrating details, preparing hearts, aligning circumstances in ways we cannot see.

The renewal of strength promised to those who wait is not merely restoration to previous levels but transformation to new capacities. It's the strength of tested faith, proven character, deepened intimacy with God. Those who have waited on God develop a quality of spirit that those who've never waited cannot possess. They have a settledness, a depth, a quiet confidence that comes from having been stretched without breaking, delayed without despairing, tested without failing.

Waiting on the Lord also teaches us about His nature in ways that immediate answers never could. We learn that He is not slow as we count slowness but patient, not wanting any to perish. We discover that His delays are not denials but often preparations for greater blessings. We find that His timing accounts for factors we cannot see, coordinates with purposes we don't understand, and aims for outcomes better than we imagined.

The eagle imagery Isaiah uses is particularly powerful. Eagles don't constantly flap their wings in exhausting effort. They wait for the right wind currents, then spread their wings and soar. They conserve energy by working with forces greater than themselves. Similarly, when we wait on the Lord, we learn to recognize His wind, to work with His timing, to soar on His strength rather than exhaust ourselves with constant flapping. This is the secret of sustained spiritual vitality—not constant striving but strategic waiting.

In practical terms, finding hope while waiting requires intentional practices. We must feed our faith with God's Word, reminding ourselves of His faithfulness throughout history. We need to maintain spiritual disciplines even when they feel dry and unproductive. We should surround ourselves with encouraging believers who can speak faith when ours falters. We must celebrate small mercies and minor progress rather than focusing only on the ultimate answer we seek. We need to serve others even while we wait, preventing our waiting from becoming self-focused and bitter.

PRAYER FOR PATIENCE IN WAITING

Eternal God, Master of time and seasons, Lord of perfect timing, I come before You from the difficult place of waiting. You know how long I've been waiting, how many times I've hoped only to be disappointed, how often I've thought breakthrough was near only to face continued delay. Lord, I confess my impatience, my frustration with Your timing, my temptation to take matters into my own hands. Forgive me for the times I've run ahead of You or lagged behind in unbelief.

Grant me the patience that comes from trusting Your perfect wisdom. Help me to remember that You see the end from the beginning, that Your delays are purposeful, that Your timing accounts for factors I cannot see. Give me grace to wait well—not with bitter resignation but with expectant hope, not with passive indifference but with active faith, not with complaining spirit but with grateful heart. Teach me to number my days in the waiting, to redeem the time, to grow in the delay rather than merely endure it.

Show me what You're doing in this season of waiting. What are You teaching me? How are You shaping me? What are You preparing me for? Help me to cooperate with Your work rather than resist it. When I'm tempted to give up, remind me of Your faithfulness. When doubt creeps in, anchor me in Your promises. When others seem to pass me by, help me to celebrate their blessings without bitterness. Let my waiting be a testimony to others of Your worthiness, showing that You are worth waiting for regardless of the outcome. In Jesus' name, Amen.

PRAYER FOR RENEWED HOPE AND TRUST

Faithful Father, God of hope, Keeper of promises, I bring before You a heart that has grown weary in waiting. My hope feels fragile, like a flickering candle in the wind. My trust has been shaken by delay after delay. I'm tired of hoping only to be disappointed, of believing only to see nothing change. Yet I know that You are faithful, that Your Word is true, that Your promises never fail, even when fulfillment seems impossibly distant.

Renew my hope, Lord, not in my circumstances changing but in You who never changes. Restore my trust, not in my ability to figure things out but in Your sovereign control over all things. Revive my faith, not in formulas or timelines but in Your character and love. Help me to hope in You rather than in specific outcomes, to trust Your heart when I cannot trace Your hand, to believe Your promises even when I don't see progress.

Fill me with the strength that comes from hoping in You. Let me soar above my circumstances on eagles' wings of faith. Enable me to run this race with endurance, fixing my eyes on Jesus, the author and perfecter of my faith. Help me to walk steadily forward even when the path seems long and the destination unclear. Transform my waiting from a season of mere endurance to a time of profound encounter with You. Let me discover in the waiting a depth of relationship with You that quick answers could never produce. Through Christ, my living hope, Amen.

REFLECTION QUESTION

What have you been waiting for that has tested your faith? How might God be using this season of waiting to develop something in you that couldn't be forged any other way?

CHAPTER 9: LIVING IN VICTORY THROUGH CHRIST'S LOVE

KEY SCRIPTURE

"No, in all these things we are more than conquerors through him who loved us. For I am convinced that neither death nor life, neither angels nor demons, neither the present nor the future, nor any powers, neither height nor depth, nor anything else in all creation, will be able to separate us from the love of God that is in Christ Jesus our Lord." (Romans 8:37-39, NIV)

DEVOTIONAL REFLECTION

These triumphant words from Paul represent one of the highest peaks of revelation in all of Scripture. Written by a man who knew suffering intimately—shipwrecks, beatings, imprisonment, betrayal, disappointment—these are not the words of naive optimism but battle-tested truth. Paul doesn't claim we won't face difficulties; instead, he declares that in the midst of them all, we are super-conquerors, hyper-victors, overwhelmingly triumphant through Christ who loved us.

The phrase "more than conquerors" deserves careful attention. A conqueror defeats their enemy and survives the battle. But we are more than conquerors—we don't merely survive our battles; we emerge from them stronger, refined, transformed. We don't just endure suffering; we triumph through it. We don't simply withstand attacks; we turn them into opportunities for greater victory. This is the mysterious mathematics of God's kingdom where subtraction leads to addition, death leads to life, and suffering leads to glory.

The foundation of this overwhelming victory is not our strength, strategy, or spirituality—it's "through him who loved us." Christ's love is not passive sentiment but active power. It's the love that left heaven's throne for earth's manger, that touched lepers and ate with sinners, that carried our cross and bore our shame, that conquered death and hell for our freedom. This love is not past tense only—Christ loved us—but continuing present reality. He loves us now, in this moment, with the same intensity that led Him to Calvary.

Paul then presents a comprehensive list of forces that might threaten to separate us from God's love. He starts with the ultimate opposites—death and life. Death, humanity's final enemy, the separation that seems most permanent, cannot separate us from God's love. But neither can life, with all its changes, challenges, and complexities. Sometimes life's difficulties can feel more threatening than death itself. Yet whether we're facing the end of life or the ongoing struggles of life, God's love remains unbreakably attached to us.

He continues with spiritual forces—angels and demons. No spiritual being, whether fallen angels seeking our destruction or even holy angels (should they somehow turn against us), can break the bond of God's love. The spiritual realm with all its mysteries and powers is subject to the supreme power of God's love for His children. The demons that accuse, attack, and attempt to destroy cannot succeed in separating us from the love that has claimed us.

The temporal dimensions are covered next—present and future. The present, with all its pressures, problems, and pain, cannot sever God's love. The future, with all its uncertainty, unknown challenges, and feared possibilities, cannot separate us from God's love. This means that nothing happening in your life right now and nothing that could happen tomorrow can break the bond between you and God's love. No present failure or future fear has that power.

Paul mentions "powers"—a term that could encompass earthly authorities, spiritual forces, or any form of power that might threaten us. In our context, these powers might include government persecution, cultural opposition, economic systems, social media campaigns, or any force that seems overwhelming. Yet none of these powers, regardless of their apparent strength, can overcome the supreme power of God's love.

The spatial dimensions are included—height and depth. Whether we're on the mountaintop of success or in the valley of despair, whether we're in the heights of spiritual experience or the depths of doubt and depression, God's love reaches us. There is no place too high for His love to reach, no depth too low for His love to find us. The psalmist echoes this truth: "If I ascend to heaven, you are there; if I make my bed in Sheol, you are there."

Finally, Paul adds a sweeping statement: "nor anything else in all creation." This is the ultimate catch-all phrase. If there's something Paul hasn't mentioned, if there's some force or circumstance he hasn't covered, it's included here. Nothing in all creation—nothing that exists—has the power to separate us from God's love in Christ Jesus. This includes our own failures, sins, and shortcomings. Even we ourselves cannot separate ourselves from God's love once we're in Christ.

Living in this victory through Christ's love transforms everything about our daily experience. When we truly grasp that we're inseparably loved, fear loses its grip. What can threaten those who cannot be separated from infinite love? When we understand we're more than conquerors, setbacks become setups for comeback stories. When we believe nothing can separate us from God's love, we can face anything with confidence.

This victory is not theoretical but intensely practical. It means that when you fail, you're still loved. When you're rejected by others, you're still accepted by God. When you lose everything earthly, you still possess everything eternal. When your body fails, your spirit can soar. When circumstances scream that God has abandoned you, faith whispers that His love holds you still. This is not positive thinking but revealed truth, not wishful hoping but assured reality.

The victory we have in Christ's love is also not dependent on our feelings. There will be days when we don't feel victorious, when we don't sense God's love, when everything seems to argue against these truths. But our victory is based on fact, not feeling. Christ's love is objective reality, not subjective experience. We are more than conquerors even when we feel defeated, inseparably loved even when we feel abandoned.

PRAYER OF GRATITUDE FOR CHRIST'S VICTORY

Victorious Savior, Conquering King, Lord of unfailing love, I come before You with a heart overflowing with gratitude for the victory You've won on my behalf. Thank You that when I was dead in my sins, You loved me. When I was Your enemy, You died for me. When I was helpless, You rescued me. When I was hopeless, You redeemed me. Your love sought me when I wasn't seeking You, found me when I was lost, and claimed me as Your own forever.

Thank You that Your victory is complete and final. Death could not hold You, hell could not contain You, and the grave could not keep You. You rose triumphant, defeating every enemy of my soul. Thank You that Your victory becomes my victory, that I am more than a conqueror through You who loved me. Thank You that this victory is not based on my performance but on Your perfect love, not on my strength but on Your finished work, not on my worthiness but on Your worth.

I praise You that nothing—absolutely nothing—can separate me from Your love. Not my worst failures, not my deepest sins, not my greatest fears, not my most painful circumstances. Your love is stronger than death, more persistent than life, more powerful than any force in heaven or earth. Thank You that I can face today and tomorrow knowing that Your love surrounds me, upholds me, and goes before me. Let my life be a living testimony to Your victorious love. Let others see in me the confidence that comes from being inseparably loved by You. In Your mighty name, Jesus, Amen.

PRAYER FOR CONFIDENCE IN GOD'S LOVE

Faithful Father, God of everlasting love, Keeper of my soul, I confess that I don't always live in the confidence of Your inseparable love. Sometimes I feel separated, abandoned, forgotten. Sometimes my failures convince me I've exhausted Your love. Sometimes my circumstances shout louder than Your promises. Forgive me for doubting what You've declared, for feeling what You've not said, for believing lies when You've spoken truth.

Today, I choose to believe and receive the truth that nothing can separate me from Your love. I reject the lie that I need to earn Your love or that I can lose it. I refuse to believe that my sins are stronger than Your grace, that my failures are final, that my mistakes have disqualified me from Your love. I choose to stand on the solid rock of Your unchanging love rather than the shifting sand of my changing feelings.

Fill me with the deep, experiential knowledge of Your love. Let it be more than theology but a living reality that transforms how I think, feel, and act. When doubts arise, remind me of the cross where Your love was proven. When fears assault, let Your perfect love cast them out. When accusations come, let the truth of Your inseparable love silence them. Help me to live with the confidence of one who is permanently, irreversibly, eternally loved. Let this confidence make me bold in faith, generous in love, and steadfast in hope. Through Jesus Christ, who is the proof and guarantee of Your love, Amen.

REFLECTION QUESTION

In what area of your life do you most struggle to believe in God's inseparable love? How would your daily thoughts and actions change if you truly lived as "more than a conqueror" in that area?

CHAPTER 10: FORGIVENESS THROUGH PRAYER

KEY SCRIPTURE

"For if you forgive other people when they sin against you, your heavenly Father will also forgive you. But if you do not forgive others their sins, your Father will not forgive your sins." (Matthew 6:14-15, NIV)

DEVOTIONAL REFLECTION

These words of Jesus present one of the most challenging and essential truths in the Christian life. Immediately following the Lord's Prayer, Jesus provides this sobering commentary that links our receiving of forgiveness directly to our extending of it. This is not a works-based salvation but rather evidence of a transformed heart. Those who have truly experienced God's forgiveness cannot help but extend it to others. Unforgiveness is incompatible with the gospel we claim to believe.

Forgiveness is perhaps the most supernatural act a human being can perform. Everything within our fallen nature cries out for justice, revenge, and vindication when we've been wronged. The wound wants to fester, the hurt wants to be nursed, the offense wants to be remembered and rehearsed. Unforgiveness feels like protection against further hurt, like maintaining some control over those who've hurt us, like exacting at least some payment for the debt they owe. Yet Jesus calls us to the radical, countercultural, seemingly impossible act of forgiveness.

The context of Jesus' teaching is crucial. He has just taught His disciples to pray, "Forgive us our debts, as we also have forgiven our debtors." The prayer itself establishes the connection between receiving and giving forgiveness. We're asking God to forgive us in the same manner that we forgive others. This should give us serious pause. Do we really want God to forgive us the way we forgive others—grudgingly, partially, conditionally, temporarily? Or do we want Him to forgive completely, freely, permanently, and generously?

The offenses that require forgiveness are countless and varied. There are the major wounds—abuse, betrayal, abandonment, adultery. There are the accumulated smaller injuries—harsh words, broken promises, neglect, indifference. There are systemic injustices—discrimination, oppression, exploitation. There are church wounds—spiritual abuse, hypocrisy, judgment, rejection. Each of these creates a debt in our emotional and spiritual ledger, a debt that cries out for payment.

The consequences of unforgiveness are devastating both spiritually and practically. Spiritually, unforgiveness blocks our relationship with God. It's like trying to receive water through a pipe clogged with bitterness. Our prayers feel hindered, our worship feels hollow, and our spiritual growth stagnates. We may maintain religious activities, but the life-giving flow of God's presence is restricted. Unforgiveness gives the enemy a foothold in our lives, legal ground from which to torment us with anger, bitterness, and resentment.

Practically, unforgiveness poisons every area of our lives. It affects our physical health—studies have shown that harboring unforgiveness contributes to heart disease, high blood pressure, and compromised immune systems. It impacts our mental health—feeding depression, anxiety, and a host of psychological struggles. It damages our relationships—not just with the person we won't forgive but with others, as bitterness leaks into all our interactions. It robs us of joy, peace, and the abundant life Jesus promised.

Yet forgiveness is not what many think it is. Forgiveness is not saying what happened was okay—it wasn't, which is why it needs forgiveness. Forgiveness is not necessarily reconciliation—you can forgive someone and still maintain appropriate boundaries. Forgiveness is not forgetting—the pain may have created permanent memories, though their sting can be removed. Forgiveness is not a feeling—it's a choice, a decision of the will that feelings eventually follow.

Forgiveness is releasing the right to revenge, canceling the debt someone owes us, and entrusting justice to God. It's choosing to absorb the pain rather than transmit it. It's deciding that the cross of Christ is sufficient payment for their sin against us, just as it is for our sins against God. Forgiveness is agreeing with God that vengeance belongs to Him and trusting Him to deal with the person and situation according to His perfect justice and mercy.

The power to forgive comes from understanding how much we've been forgiven. Jesus illustrated this in the parable of the unmerciful servant who was forgiven an unpayable debt yet refused to forgive a small debt owed to him. When we grasp the enormity of our sin against a holy God and the completeness of His forgiveness through Christ, extending forgiveness to others becomes possible, even inevitable. We forgive because we've been forgiven. We show mercy because we've received mercy. We cancel debts because our debt has been canceled.

Prayer is the pathway to forgiveness. In prayer, we bring our wounds to the Great Physician. We honestly express our hurt, anger, and desire for justice. We don't pretend it doesn't hurt or minimize the offense. But then we make the choice to forgive, speaking it aloud to God even when our emotions rebel. We may need to pray this prayer repeatedly as layers of hurt surface. Forgiveness is often a process, not a one-time event, especially for deep wounds.

The freedom that comes through forgiveness is indescribable. It's like being released from a prison we didn't realize we were in. The person who hurt us no longer controls our emotions. The past no longer dictates our present. The wound no longer defines us. We discover that forgiveness is not primarily for the benefit of the one who hurt us but for our own liberation. We reclaim the energy that was being consumed by unforgiveness and redirect it toward God's purposes.

PRAYER FOR THE STRENGTH TO FORGIVE

Merciful Father, God of infinite forgiveness, Healer of broken hearts, I come before You carrying wounds that seem too deep to heal and offenses that feel too great to forgive. You know the pain I've endured, the betrayal I've experienced, the injustice I've suffered. You see how unforgiveness has taken root in my heart, growing into bitterness that poisons my soul. Lord, I confess that in my own strength, I cannot forgive. The hurt is too deep, the wound too raw, the injustice too great.

But I remember how much You have forgiven me. My sins against You far exceed any sin against me. My debt to You was unpayable, yet You paid it in full through Christ. You forgave me completely, freely, permanently. Now You call me to extend that same forgiveness to others. I need Your supernatural strength to do what feels impossible. Fill me with Your Spirit who enables me to do what I cannot do naturally.

Give me the courage to choose forgiveness even when my feelings resist. Help me to release my right to revenge, trusting You to be the righteous judge. Enable me to pray for those who have hurt me, to bless those who have cursed me, to love those who have acted as my enemies. Transform my heart from a courtroom demanding justice to a channel of Your mercy. Let the forgiveness I extend be evidence of Your transforming work in my life. In the name of Jesus, who forgave even those who crucified Him, Amen.

PRAYER FOR RELEASING BITTERNESS AND RESENTMENT

Loving Lord, Healer of hearts, Restorer of souls, I bring before You the bitterness and resentment that have poisoned my spirit. These toxic emotions have been my companions for too long, and I recognize that they're destroying me from the inside out. I've rehearsed the offenses, nursed the wounds, and fed the anger until bitterness has become part of my identity. Lord, I'm tired of carrying this burden. I'm exhausted from the effort of maintaining these walls of resentment.

Today, I choose to release it all to You. I let go of my need to be vindicated, my desire to see them suffer, my requirement that they acknowledge what they've done. I release the person who hurt me into Your hands, trusting You to deal with them according to Your perfect wisdom. I release the situation that caused such pain, believing You can bring good even from this evil. I release my right to understand why it happened, accepting that some questions won't be answered this side of heaven.

Fill the spaces that bitterness occupied with Your love, joy, and peace. Where resentment has created deep grooves in my thinking, create new pathways of grace and gratitude.

Help me to see the person who hurt me through Your eyes—as someone broken who needs Your redemption just as I do. Transform my testimony from one of victimhood to victory, from bitterness to blessing, from resentment to redemption. Let my life demonstrate the freedom that comes through forgiveness. Through Christ, who breaks every chain, Amen.

REFLECTION QUESTION

Who do you need to forgive, and what specific hurt are you holding onto? What step can you take today to begin the process of forgiveness, even if you don't feel ready?

CHAPTER 11: FINDING GOD'S PRESENCE IN LONELINESS

KEY SCRIPTURE

"The Lord is close to the brokenhearted and saves those who are crushed in spirit." (Psalm 34:18, NIV)

DEVOTIONAL REFLECTION

Loneliness is perhaps one of the most pervasive and painful experiences of the human condition. It transcends circumstances—you can be lonely in a crowd, isolated in a marriage, disconnected in a church full of people. The ache of loneliness touches something fundamental in our being because we were created for relationship—with God and with others. Yet in our hyperconnected age, loneliness has reached epidemic proportions, revealing that connectivity and connection are not the same thing.

David's words in this psalm carry particular weight because they come from someone who knew loneliness intimately. He experienced the loneliness of being misunderstood by family, the isolation of being hunted by Saul, the solitude of leadership, and the desolation of sin's consequences. Yet through it all, he discovered a profound truth: God draws especially near to those who feel far from everyone else. The Lord doesn't observe our loneliness from a distance but comes close, intimately close, to the brokenhearted and crushed in spirit.

The promise that God is "close" uses a Hebrew word that implies breathing distance, face-to-face proximity. This is not a God who shouts encouragement from afar but One who draws so near we can feel His breath, sense His heartbeat, experience His embrace. The very condition that makes us feel most isolated—being brokenhearted, crushed in spirit—is what draws God's special attention and presence. Our loneliness becomes a meeting place with the Divine.

Loneliness takes many forms. There's the loneliness of singleness, wondering if you'll ever find a life partner, watching others pair off while you remain alone. There's the loneliness within marriage, living with someone who feels like a stranger, sharing a house but not a life. There's the loneliness of grief, when the person who understood you best is gone and no one else seems to comprehend your loss. There's the loneliness of chronic illness, feeling like your body has betrayed you and others have forgotten you.

We experience the loneliness of leadership, making decisions no one else understands, carrying burdens we can't share. The loneliness of failure, when friends distance themselves from our disgrace. The loneliness of success, discovering that achievement doesn't equal fulfillment. The loneliness of aging, as contemporaries pass away and the world moves on without us. The loneliness of being different, not fitting the mold, standing for truth in a culture that rejects it.

Technology promised to cure loneliness but has often intensified it. Social media shows us others' curated lives, making us feel more isolated in our struggles. Digital communication replaces face-to-face connection. We have hundreds of "friends" online but no one to call in crisis. We're more connected yet lonelier than ever, proving that the deepest loneliness is not the absence of people but the absence of genuine connection and understanding.

Yet Scripture reveals that loneliness can become holy ground where we encounter God in profound ways. It was in the loneliness of the wilderness that Moses met God in the burning bush. In the isolation of the cave that Elijah heard God's still small voice. In the solitude of prison that Paul received revelations of heaven. In the loneliness of Patmos that John saw the glorified Christ. Sometimes God allows loneliness not as punishment but as preparation for deeper intimacy with Him.

The spiritual dimension of loneliness often involves recognizing that our deepest loneliness is actually homesickness for heaven. We're eternal beings temporarily residing in a fallen world. The ache we feel is the gap between what we were created for and what we experience. No human relationship, no matter how fulfilling, can completely fill the God-shaped void in our hearts. Augustine was right: our hearts are restless until they find their rest in God.

Finding God's presence in loneliness requires intentional practices. First, we must be honest with God about our loneliness. David's psalms show us that God can handle our raw emotions, our questions, our complaints. We don't have to pretend we're fine when we're falling apart. God draws close to the brokenhearted, but we must acknowledge our brokenness. In prayer, we pour out our loneliness, and in the pouring out, we create space for God to pour in.

Second, we must learn to practice God's presence. Brother Lawrence discovered that he could experience God's presence as powerfully while washing dishes as while taking communion. God is always present; we're the ones who are absent. Through conscious awareness, conversational prayer throughout the day, and meditation on His attributes, we cultivate awareness of His constant companionship. The more we practice His presence, the less alone we feel.

Third, we must engage with Scripture differently in seasons of loneliness. Rather than just reading for information, we read for encounter. We approach the Bible as God's personal letter to us, hearing His voice speaking directly to our situation. The promises become personal, the commands become conversations, the stories become our story. Through His Word, God speaks into our loneliness with understanding, comfort, and hope.

Fourth, we must resist the temptation to isolate further. Loneliness often creates a vicious cycle—we feel lonely, so we withdraw, which makes us lonelier, so we withdraw more. But God often ministers to our loneliness through His people. This requires vulnerability—admitting our struggle, asking for help, receiving ministry. It means pushing through the awkwardness of reaching out, the fear of rejection, the pride that says we should be self-sufficient.

The transformation of loneliness into solitude is one of God's redemptive miracles. Loneliness is empty; solitude is full. Loneliness is isolation; solitude is intentional. Loneliness feels abandoned; solitude feels accompanied. When we bring our loneliness to God, He can transform it into sacred solitude where we experience His presence more deeply than we ever could in the noise of constant company. We discover that alone with God, we're never truly alone.

PRAYER FOR GOD'S COMFORT IN ISOLATION

Ever-present God, Faithful Companion, Friend who sticks closer than a brother, I come to You from the deep valley of loneliness. You see the ache in my heart, the emptiness that seems to expand with each passing day, the isolation that makes me wonder if anyone truly knows or cares that I exist. Lord, the loneliness is so heavy sometimes I can barely breathe. It feels like I'm invisible, forgotten, unwanted, unknown.

But Your Word promises that You are close to the brokenhearted, and my heart is truly broken. Draw near to me, Lord, in this lonely place. Let me sense Your presence in tangible ways—through Your Word that speaks directly to my situation, through unexpected blessings that remind me You see me, through Your Spirit's whisper that I am never alone. Help me to experience You as my closest friend, my constant companion, my understanding confidant.

Transform this season of loneliness into sacred encounter with You. Teach me things in this solitude that I could never learn in the crowd. Develop in me a depth of relationship with You that only comes through undistracted attention. Help me to see that You haven't abandoned me to loneliness but invited me into intimacy. Show me that this valley is not a dead end but a passage to deeper fellowship with You. When human companionship fails or falls short, be my all-sufficient friend. Remind me that even if father and mother forsake me, You will never leave me nor forsake me. In Jesus' name, Amen.

PRAYER FOR CONNECTION AND COMMUNITY

Loving Father, Creator of community, Designer of relationship, I acknowledge that You created me for connection—with You and with others. You said it is not good for man to be alone, and You know the toll that isolation takes on my soul. Lord, I ask for Your intervention in my loneliness. Provide the connections I need, the community I crave, the relationships that reflect Your love.

Open doors for meaningful friendships. Bring people into my life who understand my journey, share my values, and encourage my faith. Give me courage to be vulnerable, to reach out when I want to withdraw, to risk rejection for the possibility of connection. Help me to be the kind of friend I wish to have—available, understanding, faithful, and kind. Show me how to build bridges rather than walls, to initiate rather than wait, to give what I hope to receive.

I pray for Your church to be a true family for the lonely. Help us to notice those who sit alone, to include those on the margins, to pursue those who've drifted away. Make us a community where no one has to bear their burdens alone, where everyone has a place at the table, where the lonely find family. Use my own experience of loneliness to make me sensitive to others who are struggling with isolation. Let me be Your hands and feet to reach out to the lonely, Your voice to speak encouragement, Your heart to show compassion. Through Christ, who knew the ultimate loneliness of the cross so we would never be alone, Amen.

REFLECTION QUESTION

How has loneliness actually drawn you closer to God, and what is He teaching you in this season that you might not have learned surrounded by people?

A LIFE OF PRAYER
AND STRENGTH

As we conclude this devotional journey, we stand at what is truly a beginning—the commencement of a deeper, more intentional walk with God through prayer and spiritual warfare. These pages have been more than words; they've been an invitation into a transformed way of living, a call to take our place as warriors in God's kingdom.

Throughout these chapters, we've explored the multifaceted nature of spiritual warfare. Our battles are not against flesh and blood but against spiritual forces that require divine weapons. Victory comes not through human strength but through God's power, addressing every struggle—uncertainty, temptation, fear, unforgiveness—at its spiritual root.

We began by learning that trust is active faith, not passive resignation. This foundation underlies everything else, for without it, prayer becomes empty words and warfare becomes futile human effort. We discovered the paradox that God's strength is perfected in our weakness, revolutionizing how we approach battles. Rather than striving to be strong enough, we learned to embrace our dependence on God.

Fear no longer needs to control us when we understand that God's peace—His presence amid problems—guards our hearts and minds. Scripture became our filter against deception, our weapon in mental battles. We found shelter in the Most High's protection, though this doesn't guarantee a trouble-free life but assures that everything touching us passes through His permissive will for our ultimate good.

The freedom of releasing burdens through prayer proved to be more than sentiment—it's essential for spiritual health. We're not victims of temptation but victors through Christ, who always provides escape. Waiting revealed itself as preparation rather than denial, refining faith and deepening dependence. The truth that nothing can separate us from God's love became our foundation for victory. Forgiveness, we learned, liberates the forgiver more than the forgiven.

Moving forward, several principles guide our continued growth:

Consistency is crucial. Spiritual strength builds through daily discipline, not occasional intensity. Regular prayer and Scripture engagement in peaceful times prepare us for battles ahead.

Community is essential. We weren't designed to fight alone. The body of Christ provides support, accountability, and mutual sharpening. Isolation weakens; fellowship strengthens.

Position determines power. We fight from Christ's victory, not for it. His completed work at the cross means we're enforcing an already-won battle, not attempting to win one.

Eternal perspective transforms temporary struggles. Today's overwhelming battles become tomorrow's distant memories, but character forged through them lasts forever. Every faithful prayer and obedient act contributes to eternal glory that outweighs momentary troubles.

God's love anchors everything. The enemy's primary strategy targets this truth, attempting to convince us we're alone or unworthy. Yet we remain loved, chosen, and cherished based on Christ's work, not our performance.

Expect both opposition and transformation as you continue. Increased spiritual attacks often indicate effectiveness—the enemy doesn't waste resources on ineffective soldiers. Simultaneously, watch for growth: stronger faith, sharper discernment, deeper peace. Your responses to challenges will shift from fear to faith, anxiety to assurance.

The prayers in this devotional are templates, not conclusions. They're starting points for developing your own voice in spiritual warfare. Continue growing in honest, specific, faith-filled prayer that declares promises rather than just presenting problems.

Remember that prayer transforms us as much as our circumstances. Through it, we develop Christ's heart, perspective, and passion. The ultimate victory isn't defeating enemies but becoming like Jesus.

God has equipped us for every battle ahead. We possess His Word as our sword, His Spirit as strength, His promises as foundation, His presence as companion. We wear His armor, wield Jesus' name, and stand under the blood's protection. We are more than conquerors through Him who loved us.

The battles continue until Christ returns or calls us home. Some days bring obvious victory; others feel like defeat. Mountains will be conquered; valleys will be crossed. Through soaring and struggling, God remains faithful. His strength stays sufficient, His grace abundant, His love inseparable.

FINAL PRAYER OF BLESSING AND ENCOURAGEMENT

Almighty God, Sovereign Lord, as we conclude this devotional journey, we stand before You with grateful hearts ready for battle. Thank You for the truths You've revealed and the transformation You've begun. We recognize that this ending is truly a beginning—the start of a deeper prayer life and more effective spiritual warfare.

Lord, I pray for every person who has journeyed through these pages. Strengthen them for the battles ahead. When uncertainty comes, help them trust You completely. When weakness overwhelms, be their strength. When fear threatens, be their peace. When temptation strikes, provide escape. When waiting seems endless, renew their hope. When they need to forgive, grant them grace. Remind them always that they are more than conquerors through Christ.

Establish them as mighty warriors in Your kingdom. Let their prayers shake heaven and change earth. Let their faith inspire others to stand strong. Let their victories encourage the defeated. Make them lighthouses in darkness, fountains of hope in despair, channels of Your love in a loveless world.

Place them strategically where their prayers are most needed and their faith can make the greatest impact. Give them discernment for the battles You're calling them to fight. Provide them with prayer partners and spiritual community to strengthen their resolve.

Protect them from the enemy's counterattacks. Cover them with Your blood. Surround them with Your angels. Let no weapon formed against them prosper. When they stumble, help them rise. When they fail, restore them. Fill them afresh with Your Holy Spirit. Let Your power, love, joy, and peace flow through them unhindered.

Lord, I pray for revival that begins personally and spreads to families, churches, and nations. Use these prayer warriors to push back darkness and expand Your kingdom. Remind them daily that the battle is Yours, the victory is won, and You who began this good work will complete it.

Until faith becomes sight and every knee bows to Jesus Christ as Lord, keep them strong, faithful, and victorious.

In the mighty name of Jesus Christ our Lord, our Savior, our Conquering King, Amen.

www.ingramcontent.com/pod-product-compliance
Lightning Source LLC
Chambersburg PA
CBHW031246120626
46545CB00007B/2682